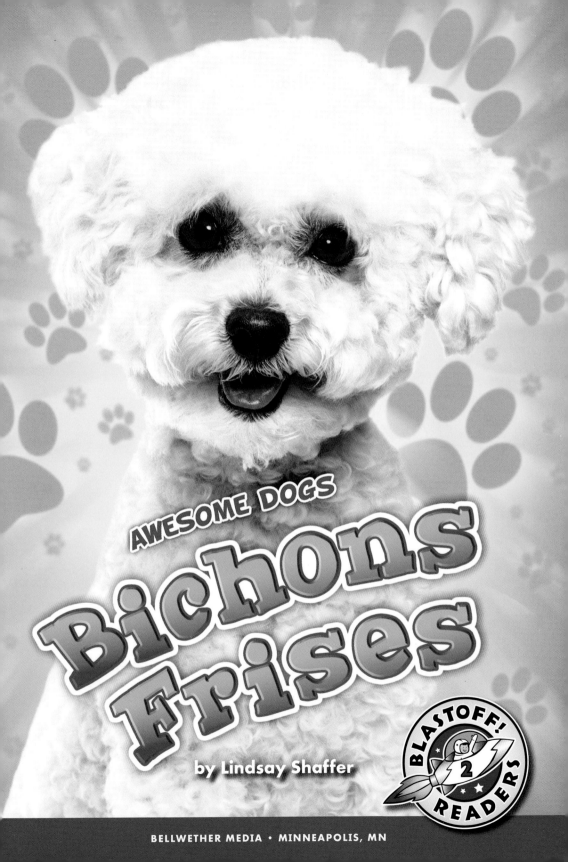

AWESOME DOGS

Bichons Frises

by Lindsay Shaffer

BELLWETHER MEDIA · MINNEAPOLIS, MN

Note to Librarians, Teachers, and Parents:

Blastoff! Readers are carefully developed by literacy experts and combine standards-based content with developmentally appropriate text.

Level 1 provides the most support through repetition of high-frequency words, light text, predictable sentence patterns, and strong visual support.

Level 2 offers early readers a bit more challenge through varied simple sentences, increased text load, and less repetition of high-frequency words.

Level 3 advances early-fluent readers toward fluency through increased text and concept load, less reliance on visuals, longer sentences, and more literary language.

Level 4 builds reading stamina by providing more text per page, increased use of punctuation, greater variation in sentence patterns, and increasingly challenging vocabulary.

Level 5 encourages children to move from "learning to read" to "reading to learn" by providing even more text, varied writing styles, and less familiar topics.

Whichever book is right for your reader, Blastoff! Readers are the perfect books to build confidence and encourage a love of reading that will last a lifetime!

This edition first published in 2019 by Bellwether Media, Inc.

No part of this publication may be reproduced in whole or in part without written permission of the publisher. For information regarding permission, write to Bellwether Media, Inc., Attention: Permissions Department, 6012 Blue Circle Drive, Minnetonka, MN 55343.

Library of Congress Cataloging-in-Publication Data

Names: Shaffer, Lindsay, author.
Title: Bichons Frises / by Lindsay Shaffer.
Description: Minneapolis, MN : Bellwether Media, Inc., 2019. | Series: Blastoff! Readers. Awesome Dogs | Audience: Age 5-8. | Audience: K to Grade 3. | Includes bibliographical references and index.
Identifiers: LCCN 2018031914 (print) | LCCN 2018037521 (ebook) | ISBN 9781681036373 (ebook) | ISBN 9781626179066 (hardcover : alk. paper)
Subjects: LCSH: Bichon frise–Juvenile literature.
Classification: LCC SF429.B52 (ebook) | LCC SF429.B52 S53 2019 (print) | DDC 636.72–dc23
LC record available at https://lccn.loc.gov/2018031914

Editor: Betsy Rathburn   Designer: Laura Sowers

Printed in the United States of America, North Mankato, MN.

Table of Contents

What Are Bichons Frises?

Bichons frises are small, **outgoing** dogs. They are loving and **confident**.

They love playing
with other dogs
and children.

Soft, Fluffy Hair

Bichons have curly white **coats**. Their tails form **plumes** above their backs.

Round, dark eyes peek out from their fluffy faces. Their ears are floppy and soft.

Bichons frises are a small **breed**. They are about 11 inches (28 centimeters) tall.

They weigh up to 18 pounds
(8 kilograms).

Bichons are **sturdy** little dogs. Strong muscles help them jump and play.

They are known for
their **tireless** energy!

Bichons frises first came from the Canary Islands in Spain.

Spain

N
W E
S

Canary Islands

Bichon Frise Profile

floppy ears

plumed tail

fluffy coat

sturdy body

Life Span: 14 to 15 years

Trainability:

1   2   3   4   5   6

Hardest to train   Easiest to train

In the 1500s, they were pets of French **royalty**. This lasted until the late 1700s.

Later, some bichons became circus dogs. They learned to do special tricks.

These playful dogs were
easy to train!

Bichons frises joined the **American Kennel Club** in 1971.

These cute pets are part of the **Non-sporting Group**.

agility course

Bichons love to have fun. They enjoy **agility** and **rally** competitions.

Owners often smile at
their cheerful nature!

Bichons are cuddly lap dogs.
They love when people pet
their soft coats.

Every day is full of fun and friends for bichons frises!

Glossary

agility—a dog sport where dogs run through a series of obstacles

American Kennel Club—an organization that keeps track of dog breeds in the United States

breed—a type of dog

coats—the hair or fur covering some animals

confident—believing that someone or something will succeed

Non-sporting Group—a group of dog breeds that do not usually hunt or work

outgoing—friendly

plumes—sections of long, fluffy fur

rally—a dog sport that focuses on obedience skills

royalty—related to kings and queens

sturdy—strongly built

tireless—without becoming tired

To Learn More

AT THE LIBRARY

Gagne, Tammy. *Bulldogs, Poodles, Dalmatians, and Other Non-sporting Dogs.* North Mankato, Minn.: Captstone Press, 2017.

Gagne, Tammy. *The Dog Encyclopedia for Kids.* North Mankato, Minn.: Capstone Young Readers, 2017.

Schuh, Mari. *Dalmatians.* Minneapolis, Minn.: Bellwether Media, 2018.

ON THE WEB

FACTSURFER

Factsurfer.com gives you a safe, fun way to find more information.

1. Go to www.factsurfer.com.

2. Enter "bichons frises" into the search box.

3. Click the "Surf" button and select your book cover to see a list of related web sites.

Index

The images in this book are reproduced through the courtesy of: Eric Isselee, front cover, p. 5; OlgaOvcharenko, pp. 4-5; Waldemar Dabrowski, p. 6; Kellymmiller73, pp. 6-7; Eudyptula, pp. 8, 14; GROSSEMY VANESSA/ Alamy, pp. 8-9; GVision, p. 10; Vladimir Nenezic, p. 11; Svetography, p. 13; MIHAI DRAGNESCU, p. 15; Tom Liska, p. 16; DGLimages, p. 17; Ivana P. Nikolic, p. 18; mikeledray, pp. 18-19; Harry & Eunae, p. 20; Mikkel Bigandt, p. 21.